Getting Your Kid to Talk

Dave Veerman

Tyndale House Publishers, Inc. • Wheaton, Illinois

To Kara and Dana, my two talkative teenagers

This book was produced with the assistance of The Livingstone Corporation

Library of Congress Cataloging-in-Publication Data

Veerman, David.
    Getting your kid to talk / David Veerman.
        p.   cm.
    ISBN 0-8423-1326-5
    1. Parent and child—United States—Miscellanea.   2. Parenting—Religious aspects—
Christianity—Miscellanea.   3. Communication in the family—United States—Miscellanea.   I. Title.
HQ755.85.V44   1994
306.874—dc20   93-35792

Printed in the United States of America

99 98 97 96 95 94
9   8   7   6   5   4   3   2

Contents

Introduction

Question: "What did you do?"
Answer: "Nothing."

Question: "How was school?"
Answer: "Okay."

If that less than sparkling conversation sounds familiar, welcome to the club of parents who find it difficult to communicate with their children. For whatever reason (lack of time, communication skills, effort, etc.), many parents struggle with getting their kids to respond with more than grunts, nods, and one-word answers. And every probing question feels like an intrusion, prying into the private life of a stranger.

Let's face it, our children are growing and changing, almost before our eyes. And they are becoming increasingly independent. They still need us, of course, but they don't necessarily feel that need very often. Thus we parents need to be creative in our efforts to break their sounds of silence.

The purpose of this book is to provide ideas for parents to use in getting their kids to talk. Because every family is unique, not all of the ideas will be for you. But some will! Check out the following entries—plus the bonus ideas!—and use what you can. Keep those communication lines open!

Around the House

Often great opportunities for talk arise around the house. Perhaps you're watching TV with your children, or maybe you're all relaxing in the family room after school and work. Or maybe everyone just happens to be home on the same evening. Use the ideas in this chapter to spark family conversations.

1 **Write to a missionary.**

Write a letter to a missionary (your church can provide a name and address). Consider sending a "care package" filled with cookies or other treats. As you write the letter and fill the box together, ask your kids some thought-provoking questions.

Here are some possible questions
- Why are missionaries needed?
- What motivates someone to become a missionary?
- What do missionaries have to learn to be able to communicate in another culture and language?
- How do you think people in your missionary's country feel about people from our country?
- What can we do to become missionaries right here?

2   **Support a child through a relief agency.**

It's especially fun if you can choose a child near the age of your children. Write to your child as a family. Ask your kids

- What would our sponsored child like to know about us?
- In what ways is his or her life like ours? In what ways is it different?
- What does he or she need the most?
- What can our family do that would make this child happy?

3 Work on crossword puzzles together.

This can be fun for one parent with one or two children—or you can divide a larger family into teams to challenge each other! Crossword puzzles obviously teach about words and their meanings. In addition, they can open up interest in lots of other areas. Bible crossword puzzles, for example, send players to the Bible to find answers. It's fun to work on crossword puzzles with someone else, because two heads are better than one.

4   **Watch a Christian video.**

High-quality Christian videos can be excellent conversation
starters if you watch them with your kids!

- **For younger children:** Kingdom Adventures, Hug-A-Long
  Songs, and Billabong Tales (Tyndale House). Each video in
  these series comes with an insert for parents to help them
  talk with their children.
- **For grades 3–6:** McGee and Me! videos (Focus on the Family
  and Tyndale House Publishers) include a discussion guide for
  parents. The Adventures in Odyssey series (Focus on the
  Family) is also good for grade-school age children.

- **For grades 5–9:** The New Adventures of McGee and Me! (Tyndale House). In these stories, Nicholas and his friends are in junior high.
- **For junior and senior highers:** *The Music Box* (Lion Pictograph), *The Love Experiment,* and many other more recent releases. *Sex, Lies, and the Truth* (Focus on the Family) should start a lively conversation with teenagers about sex and abstinence.

BONUS IDEA!

Praise your kid's choice of clothes.

5 **Read a good editorial.**

Check out the newspaper for a thought-provoking editorial or column. Clip it and give it to your son or daughter. After he or she has had a chance to read it, ask for his or her thoughts.

• What's your general impression of the column?
• Do you agree with the writer's point? Why or why not?
• Do you think most people agree with the writer? How about your friends?
• If you could write an editorial in the paper, what would you write about?

6   **Watch the network news.**

News programs or special broadcasts may provide poignant
moments or controversial incidents to talk about. You can ask

- Why did the people react that way?
- What would you do if you were in that situation?
- Where would Jesus be in that scene? What would he be
  doing? Why?
- Is there another side to the story that wasn't shown on the
  news?
- Was the news report fair to both sides?
- How can we be sure that the news report was accurate?

7   **Play board games.**

Many board games lead naturally to conversation. Word games, such as Scrabble, Boggle, or Balderdash, are especially effective. For fourth graders and older, try Sticky Situations (the McGee and Me! game). Each "sticky situation" is a typical moral or ethical dilemma faced by children ages nine to thirteen. How a player acts in the situation is determined by a roll of the die, and appropriate consequences follow. It's good to take time to talk about each situation. Older children and teenagers also enjoy the Ungame, a game where nobody loses or wins, but everybody finds out a lot about each other.

8   Put messages in balloons.

Write short messages on slips of paper. Roll up the messages and put them in balloons. Inflate the balloons and tie them off. Have the family bat the balloons around. Then, at your signal, each person should catch a balloon, pop it, and remove the message. One at a time, have each person read his or her message out loud and explain its meaning. Message suggestions: proverbs, sayings, Bible verses.

Or write questions instead of messages on the slips of paper. It's fun to get the kids involved writing the questions.

Here are some samples to get you started

- What is your favorite . . . ?
- What is your pet peeve?
- When were you happiest this morning?
- What one thing would you like to change around here?
- If you could have one wish come true, what would it be?
- What would be the first thing you would save in a fire?
- If you were an animal, what kind would you be?

Take your kid to a ball game.

9   **Rub each other the right way.**

Arrange everyone in a circle and have each person massage the
back of the person in front of him or her. After a few minutes,
have everyone turn and face the other direction and massage
that person's back.

10 **Watch a video movie.**

Believe it or not, the film industry has produced a few movies that are suitable for family viewing! These include *Anne of Green Gables, Anne of Avonlea, The Journey of Natty Gann, Savannah Smiles, Jesus of Nazareth, A.D., The Neverending Story, The Trip to Bountiful, Jacob Have I Loved, Chariots of Fire, Yentl,* and the classics *It's a Wonderful Life, Mr. Smith Goes to Washington,* and others. A valuable resource is *Video Movies Worth Watching* (Baker Book House, 1992). This book highlights about eighty films, includes warnings and suggestions for viewing, and suggests discussion questions.

11 Read a comic strip.

Find a comic strip or a cartoon that you think your son or daughter would enjoy and that makes a point (for example, "Doonesbury," "For Better or for Worse," "Funky Winkerbean," "Kudzu," or "Calvin and Hobbes"). Show the cartoon to your son or daughter, and ask what he or she thinks about it.

12 Play Bible charades.

Take turns acting out Bible characters and stories. You can do this as individuals or in teams. The team or person who guesses correctly gets to go next. During a break or after the game, comment positively on specific actions that occurred during the game.

Then ask questions like these
• Why did you choose that action to portray that person?
• Why was _____ so easy to guess?
• How do you think you would have reacted in that situation?

Here are some ideas for stories you can portray
• Adam and Eve give in to temptation

- Noah gathers all the animals
- Rebekah brings water for the camels
- Joshua and the Israelites defeat Jericho
- Ruth decides to stay with Naomi
- David defeats Goliath
- Elijah goes to heaven in a whirlwind
- Jonah spends three days in the stomach of the great fish
- Esther asks King Ahasuerus to dinner
- Mary meets the angel Gabriel
- Jesus raises Jairus's daughter
- Mary and Martha invite Jesus to dinner
- Jesus uses clay to heal a blind man
- Mary Magdalene discovers the empty tomb
- Paul is converted on the road to Damascus

BONUS IDEA!

Look your kid in the eye.

13 Make a family expression board.

Install a bulletin board in the kitchen or family room. Explain that any family member may post any news item, article, cartoon, poem, thought, etc. that he or she wants the whole family to see. After dinner or during a family time, talk about one or two of the items that have been posted.

14 Watch a television show.

You're probably disgusted with the typical television fare these days. Every sitcom seems to be filled with sexual innuendos and profanity. Occasionally a good show turns up, but we always wonder when the producer will decide to drop in an anti-Christian or immoral message. Watch TV with your kids, and be alert for conversation starters.

Some provocative questions are

- Did the leading character do the right thing?
- What would happen if he or she tried that in real life?
- Is the show fair to teachers, parents, the church?
- Why do you think violence was included?
- What do you wish would happen on this show?
- How do people get ahead on this show? money? power? good looks? brutality? How should they get ahead?
- How are women and children treated?
- Is the show's treatment of sex true to life? Is it the way life ought to be?

15 **Play a Christian tape or CD.**

Ask your son or daughter to choose a favorite Christian
recording and play it for you. Listen carefully to the words.
Afterward, you can ask

- Why do you like that song?
- What's the message—what's the artist trying to say?
- How do you feel about the message?
- How do you think you or we as a family measure up?
- What passage in the Bible relates to this topic?

BONUS IDEA!

Read one of your child's favorite
books and talk about it together.

16 Check out the sports section of the newspaper.

Choose a controversial sports story to talk about. Here are some questions it may raise:

- Why are professional athletes paid so much? How much money is enough?
- In what situations can competition be good? When is it bad?
- What causes athletes to brag, talk trash, or start fights?
- Why can't we just play games for fun?
- What does it mean to be a good sport?
- What makes a good coach?
- What makes a good team member?
- Why do people get so upset at umpires and referees?

17 Look at old photographs.

Bring out pictures of you when you were the age that your child is now. Ask:

- How do you think life was different back then? In what ways was it the same?
- From whom did you get your good looks? Dad? Mom? In what ways do you look like Grandma or Grandpa?
- Where was this picture taken? What do you remember about Grandma and Grandpa's house (the one in the picture)? Why is it fun to visit them?
- Do you think Grandma and Grandpa did an okay job in raising me?
- What kind of a parent do you think you'll be?

18 Talk about TV ads.

Many TV ads make outrageous claims. Others appeal to the viewer's feelings without explaining the benefits of the product. Many, many ads seem to promise happiness if only you buy a product. Even young kids are smart enough to detect dishonest or misguided ads. Talk back to the set and argue with the TV announcer!

Some questions to ask when you feel like arguing with the commercials

- What techniques are the advertisers using to try to sell their products?
- What's wrong with the logic in the ad? (For example, what do ads really tell us about athletic shoes? Or about luxury cars?)
- What would the advertisement say if it were truthful?
- If people buy this product, will they be happier? For how long?
- How would you advertise the Christian faith? Would your ad be attractive? Why or why not?

19 Watch family movies, videos, or slides.

Things you might talk about:
- What do you remember about that vacation (or house or neighborhood, etc.)?
- When you were that age, what did you think you would be like at your present age?
- What was the biggest challenge or problem you faced back then? How do you feel about that now?
- What would you like to do on our next vacation?
- What would you like to do that we could tape and then play back two years from now? Why?
- What's your favorite family memory? Why?

BONUS IDEA!

Don't nag about your teenager's messy room.

20 Listen to your kids when they watch the news.

Lots of kids talk back to the TV screen. "That's disgusting!"
"How can people live that way?" "I think that's wrong."
"Yuck!" "Yes!" Listen and react. You might ask

- What do you mean by that?
- Why is that wrong?
- What can we do to help that person?
- How fair are the reporters?
- If you were a reporter, how would you report what went on?

After School

When kids come home from school, especially when they don't have an after-school activity, they want to kick back and relax. If you ask, "What happened at school today?" they will probably say, "Nothing." But give them something to eat or work together with them on something totally unrelated to school, and conversation starts to flow. Check out these ideas.

21 Bake cookies together.

As you mix the batter, form the cookies, and put them in the oven, ask
- In what ways are people like chocolate chip cookies?
- If growing up is like becoming a cookie, which stage are you at—ingredients being gathered, cookie batter being stirred, cookies being formed, baking but still soft, being pulled out of the oven just right (hot and tasty) or burned and broken? Why?

22 **Share the cookies.**

Make extra cookies to wrap up and deliver as an anonymous gift to a neighbor, classmate, or friend who needs a lift. Or take a dozen cookies to a friend in a nursing home. Stay a few minutes and eat cookies together with him or her.

23 Put notes in the lunch bag.

If your child carries a lunch to school, write a note occasionally and slip it into the lunch bag secretly. Some notes should be encouraging and affirming. Some may be just for fun: a joke, a riddle, a question. When your child comes home from school, ask what he or she thought about what you wrote.

{ BONUS IDEA! }

Create a funny card together to send
to a friend or a sibling at camp.

24 **Put the child in charge.**

Give your child fifteen minutes of uninterrupted time. Tell the child that he or she is in charge for that amount of time and that you will do anything the child wants to do and talk about anything that he or she wants to talk about. If your child wants to play a game, play it. If he or she wants to take a bike ride, take it together. Let the child lead the way in the activity. Most children are very open to talking during and right after spending a few minutes in this way.

25 **Celebrate a little-known holiday.**

Decorate the kitchen and celebrate an obscure holiday, like Groundhog Day or Patriots Day or Guy Fawkes Day (or make up a holiday). Having fun together helps kids open up about school, relationships, and activities.

If you need to prime the pump, try asking

- How could we persuade Congress to make this a national holiday?
- If someone had a holiday to celebrate your birth, what would you want people to remember you for?
- People eat turkey for Thanksgiving and hot dogs on the Fourth of July. What should they eat when your birthday becomes a national holiday?
- Why do people celebrate holidays? What are holidays good for?
- What holidays should we celebrate in the future? Let's find some or make some up.

26 Work on a hobby.

Choose a hobby together and spend time on it after school. While you are working together, many opportunities for conversation will arise—especially if you, the parent, are willing to do more listening than talking. You could try stamp, coin, or baseball card collecting, bird watching, gardening, crafts, or carpentry.

BONUS IDEA!

Go to a video arcade together.

27 **Mix a milk shake in the blender.**

On a hot day, surprise your child with a milk shake after school. (On a cold day, you could make hot chocolate.) Make one for yourself, too. Sit down and enjoy your drinks together. Concentrate on listening to whatever your child feels like talking about. If he or she doesn't say anything, just relax and enjoy the quiet—and surprise him or her with another treat tomorrow. When your child feels safe and relaxed with you, he or she will begin to talk!

Conversation starters

If your child doesn't spontaneously start to talk, ask a few specific questions. Avoid "What happened at school?" and ask questions that show you've been listening, such as

- What did Mrs. Green say about your project?
- What happened when you talked to Craig about his party?
- What did the coach tell the team about the last game?
- What did kids say about your outfit?
- How's that new girl doing at making friends?
- What do we need to get for your science project?

28 **Read the Bible.**

Choose an easy-to-understand translation. Younger children will be most interested in the stories. Some good Bible books to start with: Genesis, Ruth, Esther, the first part of Daniel, Matthew, Mark, Luke, and Acts.

Some Bibles have discussion questions and notes especially for children. *The Bible for Children* is especially good for six- to twelve-year-olds. *The Life Application Bible for Students* is a gold mine for kids in junior high and above.

BONUS IDEA!

Leave a message in your
kid's computer.

29 Assemble a puzzle.

Get a jigsaw puzzle that's hard enough to challenge but not discourage your child. You may want to take your child shopping with you to help pick it out. Set the puzzle up on a small table or tray where you can work on it day after day without putting it away. Work on it together a little bit each day after school.

As you work on the puzzle together, ask questions like

- In what ways is life like a puzzle?
- What are the important pieces in life's puzzle?
- What are the missing puzzle pieces in many people's lives?
- Why is the picture on the box important to us as we try to put this puzzle together?
- What would happen if we had the wrong box?
- What kind of wrong pictures do people look at as they put their lives together?
- What are good pictures to look at as we put our lives together?
- What makes life puzzling for many kids? for you?

30 Make a patchwork quilt together.

Do this with one child or several. Get everyone involved in selecting materials, choosing the pattern, and deciding what each one's own contribution will be. While working on the quilt, let the conversation develop naturally.

Or use questions like these to get things started

- If we were sewing a quilt to represent our family, what squares would it have?
- What would you put in a quilt of your life?
- In what ways is living like sewing a quilt?
- How do the decisions we make today determine what the quilt will look like?
- Why is every person in the family important to this quilt?

31 Open the mail.

Stop! Don't throw out that junk mail! Save it and go through it with your kids. Let them open the letters and see if there's anything they want to talk about.

- Ads from stores could spark a conversation about materialism or values.
- Letters from politicians could initiate conversation on topics ranging from the federal deficit to free speech.
- Bank card mailings could begin talk about credit and spending.
- Financial pleas could stimulate thought about the real needs in the world and what can be done about them.

BONUS IDEA!

Make banana splits together on a hot day.

32 **Take pictures.**

Get a good camera and learn how to use it together. Then choose a subject to photograph. You could pick a theme such as children, animals, flowers, or old buildings. Or you could work on a family photo album.

You might want to put together a slide show to illustrate a passage of Scripture or a song. Your son or daughter could present this show at a Sunday school or a church youth meeting.

33 **Read a book together.**

It's fun to gather around while one of you reads aloud. But some families find it works better to read the same book individually and talk about it later. Check your Christian bookstore for many excellent resources. Here are a few

- **For all ages**—the seven books in the Narnia series by C. S. Lewis
- **For very young book lovers**—Christopher Churchmouse series (Davoll)
- **For fourth through seventh graders**—series fiction such as Choice Adventures (various authors), Cassie Perkins (Hunt), Elizabeth Gail (Stahl), or Mandie (Jenkins), or informative books such as *Bible Animals* (Barton et al.)

- **For junior and senior high students**—*This Present Darkness, Piercing the Darkness,* and *Prophet* (Peretti); *How to Live with Your Parents without Losing Your Mind* and *I Don't Remember Dropping the Skunk, But I Do Remember Trying to Breathe* (Davis); *The Screwtape Letters, The Great Divorce,* and the science-fiction trilogy by C. S. Lewis

34 **Look at the stamps.**

Did you toss the envelope? Pick it up and look at the stamp.
Young kids especially will enjoy this. The artwork for most
stamps has been carefully chosen—there's a story behind each
drawing.

- What do you suppose the story is?
- What do you know about the person on the stamp?
- Which stamps do you like best?
- If you were going to design your own personal stamp for all
  the letters you mail, what would it look like?

At Dinner

Although lively conversation can occur at any meal, dinner is usually the time when most of the family can be together for longer than a few minutes. During or after dinner, you can use one of these conversation starters to get the kids interacting. Make this a casual, relaxing time; you don't want the kids to feel as though they're being grilled by a police detective.

35 Play "What if . . . "

- What would you think if you heard that the entire U.S. space program was a fraud and that all those trips were actually filmed in a Hollywood studio?
- What would you do if you knew you could cure cancer, but it would cost you your life?
- What would you say if the president called to talk with you on the phone?
- What would you do if suddenly it became illegal to be a Christian?
- If you could make a new law, what would it be? Why?
- What would you do if you discovered that someone you loved dearly was a criminal?

36 Reward a secret word.

Before the meal, choose a secret word. This word should be a bit unusual, but it should be one that someone might be likely to use. Announce that you have such a word and that the first person to say it will win a prize. If no one happens to say the word during the meal, ask questions whose answers will likely include it.

Possible secret words could include

- dangerous
- intelligent
- ultimate
- grace
- morality
- agenda
- dilemma
- character
- reputation
- success
- tradition
- witness
- faith

BONUS IDEA!

Write ideas for this book together.

37 Play "Ask Anything."

This is a game that can last for several evenings. These directions will give you enough questions for five dinners.

The Preparation. Everyone gets five slips of paper. On two of these slips, kids write questions that they want Mom or Dad to answer, and parents write questions that they want the kids to answer. Collect these questions and put them in two envelopes—one marked Kids and one Parents. On the other three slips of paper, everyone writes questions that everyone should answer. Collect these and put them in an envelope marked Everybody.

The Play. During or after dinner, each person draws a question and answers it honestly. Start with the Parents and the Kids envelopes. When either category runs out, start using the Everybody questions. During the week, each person may exercise the option to "pass" one time and not answer a question that evening.

Some questions for kids to ask parents
- What did you do for fun when you were a teenager?
- How did you learn about sex?
- What was something your parents punished you for?
- What would you change about the way you were brought up?
- What was one of your biggest mistakes?
- What do you like about your kids?

Some questions for parents to ask kids
- What do you want in a friend?
- If you could choose anyone in the world, with whom would you like to have a date?
- What do you like best about yourself?
- What makes you scared?
- What would you like to change about your parents?
- What do you like about your parents?

Some questions for everyone to ask each other

- What are your goals for the next year?
- When do you feel closest to God?
- What would be a great family vacation?
- How do you like to be treated at home?
- What is your favorite food?
- What do you think heaven will be like?
- What embarrasses you the most?
- What is your pet peeve around the house?
- If you were an animal, what kind would you want to be?
- What's your favorite song? Why?
- What makes you really happy?
- What makes you proud to belong to this family?

BONUS IDEA!

Take your kid to a favorite
fast-food restaurant.

38 **Tell about your day.**

Right after saying the blessing, ask everyone to tell something that happened that day
- any one thing
- the best thing
- the most embarrassing thing
- the funniest thing

Make sure that all the other family members listen while each person is talking. It's usually a good idea to start with the youngest first and move to the oldest, ending with Mom or Dad. If a child can't think of something immediately, wait—give him or her time. Do this at every dinner. After enough practice, it will become a routine.

39 Write a continuous story.

Get a sheet of paper for each family member. Write the beginning to a story at the top of each sheet. When you give the signal, everyone (including yourself) will continue the story on the sheet of paper, writing as fast as possible. After about forty-five seconds, say, "Pass the papers." Then all papers go to the person on the right, who reads what has been written and continues the story. Continue until each story has at least five additions to it. Then shuffle the stories, redistribute them, and have each person read a story aloud.

Here are some possible story lines to use

- I thought I really knew Dad, but one day . . .
- In the middle of the night I heard . . .
- I knew it was going to be a bad day when . . .
- The menu read "Fresh Food," but I knew something was fishy when . . .
- Church has never been the same since that Sunday when . . .
- I had this crazy dream about the family. We were . . .
- Talk about weird—the other day at school . . .
- I didn't know I was scared until . . .

Any one of the stories could lead to further conversation about church, family, school, etc.

BONUS IDEA!

Compliment your kid's haircut.

40 **Look for comparisons.**

Choose an object in the room and ask how it illustrates a truth in the Christian faith. For example, you could ask

- In what ways is this tablecloth like love?
- In what ways do our eating utensils illustrate spiritual gifts?
- How might the food on our plates be compared to spiritual food?
- In what ways is our church like a family?
- How does water represent the Holy Spirit?
  Encourage the kids to look for their own comparisons.

41 Make an outrageous statement.

To catch family members by surprise, make an outrageous or unbelievable statement and see how they react. Then tell them that the statement isn't true, but continue to talk about it as though it were.

Some possible outrageous statements

- We've been spending way too much time together as a family. So from now on, we can eat only one meal a week together.
- According to a recent study, most children are more like their best friends than their parents.

- Scientists are claiming that very soon they will be able to create a complete human being by putting together parts of people who have died.
- It has been determined that the healthiest families are those in which the children tell the parents what to do.

42 Fill a verse jar.

Place a jar, some slips of paper, and a pen on the table. Explain that anyone can put the reference for a favorite Bible verse on a slip of paper and drop it into the jar. Then, periodically, draw out a slip, have someone read the verse aloud from the Bible, and lead a brief conversation about it.

{ BONUS IDEA! }

Go fishing together.

43 **Play "reverse."**

Brainstorm answers to one or more of these "reversed" questions. Then talk about what the answers imply.
- What could a person do to get a very bad reputation?
- What could we do as a family to become really poor?
- What could a teenager do to totally destroy his or her future?
- What could we do to make sure that no one found out that we were Christians?
- What could a young person do to make it through the school system but receive a terrible education?
- What could the church youth group do to be totally boring?
- What could our church do to make sure we don't grow?

44 Enforce silence.

At the beginning of the meal, announce that no one is allowed to say any words during the main meal, even to ask for food to be passed. Tell the kids that this is a game, not a punishment, and that hand signals will be allowed. Lift the ban on speaking as dessert is served. With the pent-up demand for talk, words should flow freely.

45 **Make New Year's predictions.**

Hand out paper and pens. Ask everyone to make predictions for the New Year in the following categories: world affairs, politics, sports, school, family, church, and self. Go around the table with each person sharing what he or she wrote for each of the categories. After everyone has shared all their predictions, collect the papers and save them for next December 31 when you'll review everyone's accuracy.

46 Use word pictures.

Have everyone finish statements like the ones below by
choosing a word picture to express their meaning. Word
pictures could include animals, plants, appliances, insects,
buildings, etc. Here are some sample statements:

- When our family is together, we are like a . . .
- When I get up in the morning, I am like a . . .
- Sunday morning our church is like a . . .
- When I am frightened, I feel like a . . .
- Most days I feel like a . . .
- I want my home to be like a . . .
- God is like a . . .

47 Have a meal from another country.

Choose a country and build a meal around it.

- Serve typical foods of that country.
- Wear costumes if appropriate.
- Put pictures of the country on the wall.
- Use words from that country's language (or try to imitate their accent if their language is English).
- Play music from that country.
- Celebrate one of the country's holidays.

This is all much more fun if the kids help plan and prepare. Then, when you have the meal, everyone will know enough about the country to be able to talk about what it is like and what it would be like to live there.

BONUS IDEA!

Watch your kid's favorite TV show together.

48 **Take a family survey.**

Explain that you are from a national polling organization and are taking a family opinion survey. Ask the following questions or other questions that you like better (you answer the questions, too, or the data won't be valid). After everyone has finished, total the answers for each question and divide by the number of family members to arrive at your "family data." Talk about the questions, the process, and whether the "data" accurately reflects your family.

Some questions for your survey
• How old are you?
• What is the perfect age to be?

- How many times do you expect to "fall in love" in your lifetime?
- What's the ideal number of people in a family?
- How much allowance should each child in our family receive each week?
- At what age does "old" begin?
- How old were you when you trusted Christ as your Savior?
- At what age should a young person be allowed to date?

49 Ask questions about school.

- Who is the most unpopular person at school? What makes him or her so unlikeable?
- If you could trade places with anyone in your school, what person would you choose? Why?
- If I were to interview a hundred kids your age, how many do you think would be happier than you? Why?

50 Dream a little.

Ask the family to dream. Ask
- If you suddenly had 10 million dollars, what would you do?
- How would you decide how to spend it?
- How much of it would you share with others?
- Who would you share it with?
- Would you be happier with 10 million dollars than you are today?
- Are there any ways you might be less happy?
- Is there anything you would want to do with 10 million dollars that you could start saving for today?

51 **Take a trip down memory lane.**

Ask, "Can you remember . . . ?" and recall a humorous, meaningful, controversial, poignant, or traumatic incident from the past. For example, "Can you remember . . ."

- when Mom announced she was pregnant?
- when Dad got us lost on his famous "shortcut"?
- when we overslept and missed our flight home?
- when Cindi almost drowned?
- our first day in this house?
- what you were doing when you heard that _____ had died?
- our neighbors in our first neighborhood?
- the best Christmas we ever had?

Memorize a Bible verse together.

52 **Fill a question basket.**

In the center of your table, place a small basket. Next to the basket place a stack of index cards and a pen. Explain that during the week, everyone may write questions and put them in the basket. These questions may be for the whole family or for specific individuals to answer. Then at a regular time during the week (for example, after Sunday dinner) or whenever you think the time is right, draw out a card for the group or individual to answer.

53 Ask questions for individuals or the whole family to answer.

- At youth group, with whom do you get along best?
- Describe a perfect day.
- What can I do to be a better parent?
- If you could live anywhere in the world, where would it be? Why?
- What's the most difficult thing to understand about God?
- What was your most embarrassing moment this week?
- What activity makes you happy and relaxed?

54 **Make a wish list.**

Write a series of sentence fragments like the ones below on sheets of paper.

- I wish I had . . .
- I wish I could . . .
- I wish I owned . . .
- I wish I were . . .
- I wish I knew . . .

Distribute the sheets and have everyone fill them out. Then talk about everyone's answers, one at a time.

On Weekends

Life seems to be moving at a faster pace each day. Weekends are jammed with sports, church, and other activities. Still, Friday nights and Saturdays may have pockets of unscheduled time that you can fill with a fun activity, whether with just one son or daughter or with the whole family. Use these activities to build bridges to significant conversations and deeper relationships.

BONUS IDEA!

Drive your kid to a friend's house across town.

55 **Do pantomimes.**

This is something like role play, but no talking is allowed. (Trust me: There will be lots of talk afterward.) Put five or ten situations on cards and place them in an envelope. Take turns drawing out a situation and acting it out silently for the rest of the family. Whoever guesses it correctly gets to act out the next situation. Or just take turns.

Some pantomimes you might like to try

- Someone trying to convince a friend to go bowling with him or her (play both parts)
- A parent trying to get a baby with colic to go back to sleep (2:30 A.M.)
- A student trying to stay awake and pay attention during a very boring class
- A boy (or girl) trying to impress a girl (or boy) on their first date in a restaurant—but everything seems to go wrong
- A waitress (waiter) trying to carry five orders of food from the kitchen, but chairs, customers, etc. keep getting in her (his) way
- A fisherman struggling to land the big one, but at the last second watching it get away

56 **Go on a bike trip.**

Take a family bike ride. End up at a place where you can eat lunch or have a snack together. Kids usually are open to talk after thirty minutes or an hour of not talking while riding. Also, they may want to talk about something they saw or something that happened on the trip. You could ask: "What were you thinking about on the trip today?" or "What did you think about _____[something you saw as you rode]?" Or you may just want to sit back and listen to the kids.

57 **Make a video.**

Ask your kids to help you make a video. Make sure that the topic lends itself to starring roles for the kids! Topics could include

- a mystery (for example, "The Case of the Missing Dog")
- a documentary (for example, "A Tour of the Veerman House")
- a TV special (for example, a series of interviews with celebrities [kids dressed up])
- a sitcom
- a music video

Play the video for the whole family—and then send it to the grandparents!

BONUS IDEA!

Collect the same items (for example,
baseball cards, coins, stamps).

58 Go to a movie.

Look for high-quality, thought-provoking films. Go with the whole family, or take your son or daughter on a special "date." After the movie, go out to eat and talk about it together.

An excellent resource for finding good films is *Preview: Family Movie Guide.* Published twice monthly by Movie Morality Ministry (1309 Seminole Dr., Richardson, Texas 75080/ 214-231-9910), this helpful newsletter reviews all the latest movies, evaluates them from a Christian perspective, and gives suggestions for using each film as a conversation starter.

59 Reverse roles.

Act out parents and children reversing their usual roles. After each role play, talk about what was said and done. Anything that might happen in your family can be a good subject for role play. Conversation will be especially good if you role-play something parents and kids are currently disagreeing about!

Some reversed-role situations

- A teenager (played by a parent) comes home after curfew and is confronted by a parent (played by a teenager).
- Two parents (played by kids) talk about how they should discipline their child.
- A parent (played by a child) counsels a child (played by a parent) about the opposite sex.
- A father (played by a son or daughter) tries to hold a family meeting to talk about where the family will go on vacation (another child plays the mother and the rest of the family members play the children).
- Mom and Dad (played by kids) talk to a child (played by an adult) about improving his or her performance at school.

60 **Work in the yard.**

Although many kids avoid yardwork like the plague, you may be able to get them to work joyfully if you choose a project you can tackle together. Working together provides opportunities for conversation—about the project, and also about creation, God's handiwork, pollution and the environment, and other related topics. Plant tulip and daffodil bulbs in the late fall, and in the spring when they emerge as flowers, you may find yourself talking about faith and hope!

BONUS IDEA!

Plant and tend a garden together.

61 **Visit a pet store.**

Take your son or daughter to a pet store and look at the different animals there. A store where you can actually pet animals is especially exciting for younger children. Most kids love animals and like to talk about their favorites. (Warning: Do not try this exercise if you are unalterably opposed to having a pet in your home!)

After visiting the store, you can ask

- Which pet was your favorite today?
- What was the funniest looking animal you saw?
- Which are better, dogs or cats?
- What did you see that you would definitely *not* want to have around the house?
- Why did God make so many kinds of fish?
- Why do people like to have pets?
- What's a good reason for getting a pet? What's a bad reason?
- Were the animals getting good care?
- What are the characteristics of a good pet owner?

62 **Have a treasure hunt.**

This takes some time to set up, but it can be worth it. Hide a
treasure in your yard or in a nearby park. Then write a series of
clues that progressively lead to the treasure. If you're really
ambitious, make a separate set of clues for each participant.
Bring the family together and explain the object of the game
and the rules. Then give each person the first clue and let the
hunt begin. The treasure could be a certificate for an extra treat
when you take everyone out for ice cream after the hunt is
over. Let another person hide the treasure and write the clues
for the next hunt—make it a tradition.

BONUS IDEA!

Share a bowl of popcorn.

63 Act out Bible characters.

Place the names of ten or twenty familiar Bible characters in an envelope. Have each person draw one out. Then have each person act out the character and see who can identify him or her. The object is to get people to identify the character—not to make it difficult!

Here are some characters you might want to choose from

- Adam
- Eve
- Noah
- Abraham
- Sarah
- Isaac
- Rebekah
- Jacob

- Rachel
- Leah
- Joseph
- Moses
- Miriam
- Joshua
- Rahab
- Samson

- Ruth
- Saul
- David
- Solomon
- Elijah
- Esther
- Mary

- John the Baptist
- Mary of Bethany
- Martha
- Peter
- Judas
- Paul
- Dorcas

64 **Look for clues.**

Take a walk in the park or around the neighborhood with your family, the kids, or just one son or daughter. As you walk, try to look for clues or evidence for one or two of these realities:

- the existence of God
- sin
- God's love
- human love

- grace
- human suffering
- forgiveness
- renewal

Suggestion: If you choose something negative like *sin*, pair it with something positive like *forgiveness*.

65 **Put on a play.**

Young children enjoy choosing a favorite story, assigning roles, and acting it out. With older kids, get a book of short plays at the Christian bookstore and choose one that looks thought provoking and fun. Obviously, you'll need to choose stories or plays that have the same number of characters as you have family members (unless individuals play more than one role). Consult with your pastor—you may be able to put it on in a church service.

After Church

Instead of quickly moving into afternoon activities and forgetting what happened in the morning at church, spend time afterward (driving home, during Sunday dinner, relaxing at home) talking it over. The following ideas and questions will help get you started.

66 Sing a song from the service.

Lead the family in one of their favorite hymns, choruses, or praise songs from the worship service. The kids may be more eager to join in if they choose the song. Afterward, talk about the meaning of the words and why the song was written. Ask the kids what the song says to them.

67 **Talk about the sermon.**

To talk about the pastor's sermon, ask

- Who can remember one thing the pastor said?
- What was the main point (big idea) of the sermon?
- On what passage of Scripture was the message based?
- What was the application? In other words, what suggestions did the pastor give for how we should act as a result of what he showed us in God's Word?

{ BONUS IDEA! }

Write a story together.

68 **Have a trivia contest.**

Take turns asking questions about details in the service. For
example, you could ask

- What color was the pastor's tie?
- What song did the soloist sing?
- Who was sitting in the row directly in front of us?
- What were the final words in the service?
- What were the main prayer requests?
- What did the banner in front of the sanctuary say?
- What was the third point in the pastor's sermon?

Better yet, give the kids pencil and paper during church and
have them make up trivia questions to ask each other
afterward.

69 **Pray together.**

Review the prayer requests mentioned in Sunday school and the worship service. Add others that family members might have. Have everyone make a prayer list to use during the week, then spend a few minutes praying for the requests on the list.

70 **Brainstorm sermon topics.**

Have the family pretend that they are a select task force given
the assignment of choosing the pastor's sermon topics for the
next year. Then spend a few minutes brainstorming what the
pastor should talk about. To trigger ideas, think in categories,
such as

- personal needs
- important Bible truths
- Bible characters
- teachings of Jesus
- church needs
- Christian character traits
- Christian behavior
- Bible passages

71 **Write a Scripture song or praise song.**

Most of the popular Scripture songs or praise songs are very simple. In fact, their simplicity is one reason for their popularity. Choose a favorite Bible verse or praise statement about God and put it to music. That can become your family's song. If your kids are older, have each person create his or her own song.

BONUS IDEA!

Take a bike ride together.

72   **Teach the lesson.**

Have children take turns teaching the rest of the family what they learned in Sunday school. If they have Sunday school papers, they can read from them as they teach. Older children can summarize the lesson and ask application questions. Parents should also take their turns.

73 **Explain to a friend.**

Take turns role-playing how you would explain the main point of the sermon to a good friend who doesn't attend your church. Talk about why different family members explain it in different ways.

- Is it because the people in the family are different from each other?
- Is it because you are thinking of different friends with different needs?
- Is it because the sermon has many different applications? If children didn't understand the sermon, explain it to them in terms that they can understand.

74 **Review the Scripture passage.**

Have someone read aloud a verse of Scripture from the pastor's sermon or a Sunday school class. Have someone else read and explain the context of the verse in the Bible. Together talk about what the text means and how we should apply it to our lives.

75 Ask God questions.

Give everyone an index card and a pen. Tell them to write down a question that they would like to ask God if they could. Collect the cards and read the questions aloud. Decide together what you, as a family, can do to find answers to the questions.

- Are there some you should talk about right now?
- Are there some that your pastor could help you with?
- Do you know of books that would help you to find answers to some?
- Are there some that will have to wait until you can ask Jesus face to face?

In the Car

Whether you're on vacation or just driving to Grandma's house for the weekend, an extended period of time in the car together can be a great opportunity for conversation, especially when everyone's tired of listening to the baseball game on the radio. To initiate conversation, begin by playing one of the games described below. Then bridge into talking about something that happened during the game and let the discussion take off from there. Or simply ask some of the questions listed. Make the drive interesting!

76 **Change navigators.**

When you are at a place where any of two or more routes would be satisfactory, let your child be the navigator. Show the child where you are on the map and where you want to go. Talk about the relative advantages and disadvantages of the two or three choices. Then let him or her choose the route. Do not agree or disagree; just say, "You're the navigator." Along the way, the child keeps track of where you are on the map so that he or she can guide the family safely to your destination. As the driver and navigator communicate about the trip, conversation may turn to other matters as well.

77 **Play Travel Trivia.**

This game requires two teams (males against females? front seat against back seat? parents against kids?) or two players. One side thinks of a trivia question about something related to the trip. If the other side gives the correct answer within sixty seconds, without any clues, they get ten points. If they need one clue to get the correct answer, they get five points. If they need two clues, they get two points. If they answer correctly within two minutes, they get another question and another chance to earn points. If they can't answer within two minutes, they lose their turn and must ask the other side a question.

Some sample Travel Trivia questions

- Why was Dad so upset last Tuesday?
- What animals were on the large billboard, just across the road from our motel two nights ago?
- What was our waitress's name at the restaurant last night?
- In what city did we stop for gas three days ago?
- What did Jason have for dessert yesterday in Omaha?
- What television show did we watch the first night?
- What is Denver's slogan?
- What colors are Pennsylvania's license plates?
- How long did it take to get from Chicago to Detroit?
- What brand is our tent?
- What was the speed limit in downtown Dixon?

BONUS IDEA!

Go camping together.

78 Use your imaginations.

When you go through a city or town, ask your kids to imagine what it would be like to live there.

- In what ways would it be different from where we live?
- What do you think kids in this area do for fun?
- If we lived here, in what kind of house would we live?
- How would you feel if you learned that we had to move here next month? Why?
- What would you do to prepare to move?
- What kinds of problems do the kids who live here have?
- Find a house you'd like to live in. What do you like about it?
- What kind of work could grown-ups do in this town?
- Where would we go to church?

79 Have a scavenger hunt.

Before the trip, make copies of a list of things to find while traveling. Tape each copy to a piece of cardboard so that it will be easy to write on. Give everyone a list and a pen and explain the rules.

- All the items must be outside the car.
- They must see each item before they may check it off their list.
- They must check it off immediately after seeing it (they aren't allowed to think back about what they think they remember having seen).
- When the list calls for writing down a phrase, they should write it exactly as they see it. Award a prize to whoever gets

all the items first or to whoever has the most at the end of
your time limit.

Some possible items for your scavenger list

- a tractor
- a license plate with the letter *X* in it
- a phrase about family (write it down)
- a picture of a liquid (what is it?)
- a book title (write it down)
- a pet (what kind?)
- the first name of a friend of yours (who?)
- a railroad-crossing sign
- a warning sign (which?)
- one of your favorite foods (a picture or the real thing—which food?)
- a steeple
- a cemetery
- road kill
- something pink
- something that reminds you of a Bible verse (which one? why?)
- something that reminds you of a pleasant memory (what? which memory?)

Teach your kid a skill.

80 Do license-plate math.

- Give everyone a number (for example, 22, 13, 45, 31, 8) and see who can find a license plate where the individual numbers add up to the number he or she was given.

- For more advanced players, give larger numbers and allow the players to add individual numbers and combinations together. (For example, a license plate with the numbers 13572 could add up to 18 by adding each numeral individually; 72 by adding 13, 57, and 2; 207 by adding 135 and 72; and 13,572 by putting all the numbers together.)

81 Listen to the radio.

Let your teen choose the radio station. Listen carefully to the songs. Take note when a song is played that your son or daughter seems to like (singing along is a good indication). Afterward, ask what he or she likes about the song, why it's popular, etc. If there is an interesting line about friendship, love, or social concern, ask what the words mean and what might motivate the songwriter to include them. (**Warning:** This is not the time to criticize the music or words. Also, don't ask about lyrics that might put your teenager on the defensive.)

82 Talk about youth culture.

To learn about your teenage son or daughter's culture, ask

- What are the popular music groups these days? What makes them popular?
- What television shows and movies do kids like?
- What do most kids do on the weekend for fun?
- What are the hot styles for guys? for girls?
- What words are being used a lot? Which are out of date?

83 **Play a tape.**

Before the trip, go to the Christian bookstore and buy a tape of a best-selling contemporary Christian musician. (Be sure this is a tape that your kids do not already own!) Surprise them by pulling it out and playing it. When it's over, they'll probably start to talk about it. If they don't, you can ask them if they'd mind reading the lyrics aloud from the insert in the cassette case. If you're like most parents, you didn't understand the words the first time through anyway—so your kids can do you a real favor this way!

Some questions to help you talk about the tape

- What do you think of this tape?
- The salesperson at the store told me that it's one of the hottest-selling ones in the store. Why do you think this person (or group) is so popular?
- (Choose a song with especially poignant or profound lyrics.) What do you think of the words to this song?
- Why do you think some adults have trouble enjoying or understanding teenage music?
- What could we adults do to understand it better?

84 Look for evidence.

Pretend you are a group of detectives. Explain that a crime has been committed and that your group's job is to gather evidence. After you describe the crime, they should look outside for evidence of the crime and the perpetrator.

Here are some crimes to solve

- A master thief has been stealing large buildings.
- An entire town has disappeared—it used to be in this area.
- A foreign agent has been sabotaging efforts to beautify the country.
- Someone is trying to remove all hints of Christianity from the culture.

BONUS IDEA!

Take pictures together.

85 Play "word search."

Give family members a word to search for in billboards, car license plates, store windows, and other signs along the highway. Whoever finds the word first wins 100 points and gets to ask anyone in the car a question using that word. The first person to get 1,000 points wins a prize.

Here are some possible words to use

- love
- quality
- integrity
- best
- trust

- future
- vacation
- dream
- friend
- improved

- begin
- liberty
- life
- free
- super

86 Talk about school.

To learn about a junior high school or a high school, ask

- What groups are in your school? When I was in high school, some of our groups were rah rahs, jocks, and burnouts. Who do kids hang around with these days?
- Who's the "in crowd" at school?
- In what ways are things different today from when I was in high school?
- What group(s) of people at your school do you have trouble relating to?
- Who is the most popular teacher in your school? What makes him or her so popular?
- If you were the principal, what changes would you make?

87 Add a word.

Begin a sentence and have everyone take turns adding a word as you go around the car. The idea is to keep the sentence going, using correct grammatical construction, even if the sentence makes no sense. For a more advanced version, also give a topic as you begin the sentence. You could say, for example, "The topic is church, and I begin the sentence with 'Last time . . . '"

88 Name that tune.

Turn on the radio. Turn to a station where a song is playing and see who can guess the correct name of the song first. Then turn to another station. Switch among stations with a variety of musical styles (rock, light, country, easy listening, classical, Christian, etc.). The winner is the person who is the first to identify five songs. After playing the game, talk about the differences in music between the generations, why certain songs are easier to remember than others, why different styles of music appeal to different people, and so forth.

89 Look for car clues.

As you slowly gain on a car and then pass it, ask the family to try to imagine what the people in the other car are like and where they might be going. They should look for clues on the outside and inside of the other car.

BONUS IDEA!

Sing a duet.

90 **Start a story.**

Begin a story. Go around the car and give each person ten seconds to add to the story, picking up where the last person left off. Story beginnings could include

- Once upon a time, a family was traveling . . .
- The most memorable family vacation I remember was . . .
- It was the weirdest thing. We were just driving down the road when . . .
- My ideal trip would be . . .
- It was a dark and stormy night. Suddenly the car began to make a funny sound. . . .
- The hitchhiker looked innocent and friendly, so I . . .

91 Ask fun questions.

Have fun with the following questions:
- If you could have any car, what kind would you choose? Why?
- What is the policeman following us thinking?
- In what ways does this area remind you of home?
- Of what book does this area remind you?
- If Jesus came to this area, where would he live? What would he do for a living? Where do you think he would find his disciples?
- What person from the past does this area remind you of? Why?
- What Bible verse does this place remind you of?

92 **Look for the signs.**

Each person chooses a road sign and explains how that sign can illustrate an important truth about life.

93 Make a rhyming poem.

Give the family a word. Ask each person in the car to add one line to a poem with the last word rhyming with the one you gave. When it comes back to you, add your own line and then give them the next word. (You may want to ask someone to be the scribe and write these poems down.) Use words that are easy to rhyme with. Possibilities: *day, go, met, late, me, cat, tow, eye, moo.*

94 **Create a mystery.**

Look for an interesting building. Tell everyone to use their imagination and together create a mystery story involving that building. The building could be an old church, a grain elevator, a shack, a mansion, the caretaker's house at a cemetery, a boarded-up store, etc.

95 Talk about billboards.

Pick out a billboard and ask
- What techniques is the advertiser using to try to get us to buy the product?
- Are you more or less interested in that product because of the ad? Why?
- What kind of advertisement would you like to put on a billboard along a busy highway? Why?
- If you were visiting from another planet, what would you learn about our society and culture from reading the advertisements along this highway?
- What ads do you think are most effective? Why?

Additional titles from Dave Veerman

**GETTING YOUR HUSBAND
TO TALK**   *(New! Spring 1994)*
With Gail Veerman   0-8423-1325-7
100+ ideas to get conversations
going with your husband.

FROM DAD WITH LOVE
(New! Spring 1994)
With Chuck Aycock   0-8423-1333-8
Raise confident kids by giving them
priceless, character-building gifts.

HOW TO APPLY THE BIBLE
0-8423-1384-2
Proven techniques for applying
God's Word—based on the *Life
Application Bible*.

**THE ONE YEAR BIBLE
MEMORY BOOK FOR
FAMILIES**   0-8423-1387-7
Daily verses, review questions, and
notes help families memorize and
understand Scripture.